Emotional Abuse Breakthrough Scripts:
107 Empowering Responses and Boundaries to Use with Your Abuser

Barrie Davenport

Disclaimer

No part of this publication may be reproduced or transmitted in any form or by any means, mechanical or electronic, including photocopying or recording, or by any information storage and retrieval system, or transmitted by email without permission in writing from the publisher.

While all attempts have been made to verify the information provided in this publication, neither the author nor the publisher assumes any responsibility for errors, omissions, or contrary interpretations of the subject matter herein.

This book is for entertainment purposes only. The views expressed are those of the author alone, and should not be taken as expert instruction or commands. The reader is responsible for his or her own actions.

Adherence to all applicable laws and regulations, including international, federal, state, and local governing professional licensing, business practices, advertising, and all other aspects of doing business in

Your Free Gift

As a way of saying thank you for your purchase, please begin this book by taking my Emotional Abuse Test to help you clarify if you are in an emotionally abusive relationship. Many people are confused about whether or not certain behaviors qualify as abusive. This assessment covers the specific behaviors and language that emotional abusers use consistently.

You can download your assessment and get your personal score by going to this site:

http://liveboldandbloom.com/book-test

Contents

About Barrie Davenport

Barrie Davenport is a certified personal coach, thought leader, author, and creator of several online courses on emotional abuse, self-confidence, life passion, habit creation, and self-publishing.

She is the founder of two top-ranked personal development sites, LiveBoldandBloom.com and BarrieDavenport.com. Her work as a coach, blogger, and author is focused on offering people practical strategies for living happier, more successful, and more mindful lives. She utilizes time-tested, evidence based, action-oriented principles and methods to create real and measurable results for self-improvement.

You can learn more about Barrie on her Amazon author page at barriedavenport.com/author.

Introduction

Disbelief. Confusion. Fear. Anxiety. Constant stress. Frozen feelings. Depression. Mental exhaustion. Anger. Heartache. Hopelessness.

These are just a few of the emotions expressed by victims of emotional abuse in a survey I conducted on the topic of emotional abuse in intimate relationships. You may be experiencing many of these same feelings. You may feel trapped, isolated, and unsure about how to deal with this person who is supposed to love and honor you.

What began as an exciting, loving romance has devolved into a hellish, unpredictable, unhappy coexistence in which one partner has all the power and control and the other is simply struggling to cope.

Constant low-level anxiety, that feeling of tiptoeing around on eggshells, is an all-too-common emotion with victims of emotional abuse. You don't know when your partner will erupt or what will set him or her off. Things seemed fine yesterday, but today he or she is giving you the cold shoulder for no apparent reason.

You feel off-balance and insecure because nothing is predictable with this person. In fact, you're frequently caught off-guard by the abuser's mercurial behaviors, not knowing how to respond or feeling too intimidated to speak up for yourself.

As a result, you remain in a state of hypervigilance, watching and waiting, knowing that the good mood won't last. Even calm periods make you anxious, because they always precede a storm that rips away any sense of inner peace and serenity in your own home.

In more long-term or serious cases of emotional abuse, those in which a partner verbally threatens or intimidates, anxiety turns into a cold-sweat, cowering-in-the-corner fear. Even if the abuser hasn't physically harmed you, the message is loud and clear: "If you step out of line, you'll pay for it— and it won't be pretty." These veiled threats suggest the possibility of traumatizing consequences that the victim doesn't want to invite.

By the time an emotional abuser has had a few years with you, your confidence and self-esteem have been systematically stripped away. Perhaps your self-identity has been stolen as well. You have shifted from trying so hard to make things work to struggling to keep it together through a gauze of despair and hopelessness. You just want to make it through the day without a major blowup, without the kids seeing you cry or fight, without getting yelled at, put down, or mocked.

Even if your abuser has never laid a hand on you, you feel threatened and trapped. Maybe you've come to believe that you're to blame for this mess. Maybe you believe the cruel and critical things your abuser spews at you during his or her tirades. Maybe you're so worn out with it all that you just don't give a damn any more. You're numb and detached, so it doesn't matter what he or she says or does.

When you get to this point in an emotionally abusive relationship, the idea of "standing up" to your abuser seems overwhelming. More than that—it feels downright frightening. He or she has made it clear that any pushback from you will only make things worse. The yelling and control escalates; the putdowns become more hurtful and offensive.

So you back down. You comply. You try to keep the peace for the sake of the children, for the sake of the peace in your home, for the sake of the marriage. In these intense moments, you don't realize all you are compromising by keeping the "peace." When you back down, when you don't call her out, when you give him another pass, you are further empowering your abuser. You are telling him or her, "I'm really OK with you saying and doing these things."

Please don't get me wrong here. I'm not suggesting that you are weak, that you're inviting abuse, or that you are at fault in any way. Your abuser is at fault. Your abuser is making choices to hurt you and your children and to desecrate your relationship. None of that is on you.
What I am saying is that emotional abusers wear you down to a nub. They wear you down to the

3

point that you have no emotional energy left, so you are forced to take the path of least resistance—and that path is backing down. It's what most abuse victims do to cope. But it doesn't have to be this way.

I want you to take a deep breath here and ponder these questions carefully.

- Do you have a tiny pocket of confidence, self-esteem, and strength within you?

- Do you have a small reservoir of anger and indignation that you can draw from?

- Is there any part of you that thinks, "I'm mad as hell, and I'm not going to take it any more"?

However small it may be, this feeling is your place of power, and it's from this tiny spark that you can exponentially improve your fortitude and confidence. As you learn to speak up for yourself, establish boundaries, and demand respect, you'll find your confidence grows stronger every day.

Even if you can't change your abuser's behaviors, words, and frame of mind, you can transform yourself. You can regain your identity, your self-esteem, and much of your personal power. Depending on your eventual choices (to stay in the relationship or leave it) and on your abuser's willingness to change, it's possible to reclaim your personal power and even transform your relationship. Or you can create a new relationship with a more healthy-minded, loving partner. It all begins with self-empowerment.

Baby Steps to Empowerment

If any of these suggestions are making you hyperventilate, please relax. All change begins with baby steps, and your ability to stand up for yourself and manage (or end) emotional abuse will begin the same way. You start small and build on your successes.

People who have phobias, like a fear of flying, for example, are often treated with something called cognitive behavioral therapy (CBT). Phobias are "reflexive" emotional reactions, the fight-or-flight response that arises during situations that may be safe but hold the potential for risk.

Once a phobia develops, a natural response is avoidance or escape. This may help in the short term by providing immediate relief, but it causes considerable problems in the long run by preventing you from living a full and happy life. Avoidance blocks your brain's ability to learn that the feared situations are not as dangerous as you think. It also prevents you from learning skills to manage these situations, so you can become more effective in your own life.

A valuable tool used as part of CBT is exposure therapy. The person experiencing the phobia is incrementally exposed to the fearful situation, starting with moderately stressful scenarios. With each successive step, the person builds his emotional strength and confidence. For example, someone with a fear of flying might first take a drive to the airport. Then he might sit in a flight simulator. Later on, he might take a short flight, eventually followed by a much longer flight, until he loosens the grip of fear and realizes he is safe flying in airplanes.

This exposure strategy is how you will begin by loosening the grip of your "abuser phobia." You will start with small expressions of confidence and push back with your abuser. As you feel stronger, you'll be able to set stronger boundaries for yourself, establish real consequences, and operate from a place of knowledge and strength rather than fear and confusion.

Understanding the Bully

In the previous section, I mentioned that, "Avoidance blocks your brain's ability to learn that the feared situations are not as dangerous as you think." I'm sure your feared situation (your partner abusing you) feels dangerous and scary.

Maybe your physical safety isn't at risk, but certainly your financial security, your reputation, your peace of mind, your mental health, and many other factors are potentially in peril if you anger your abuser or stand up for yourself. But let's examine these fearful feelings more closely.

Most emotional abusers are bullies, and bullies are all about perception. They might threaten. They might control. They might manipulate. But quite often, if you call them out on their behaviors, if you expose them for who they really are, they back down. Many emotional abusers suffer from the same low self-esteem and lack of confidence that you do. As you get stronger, they might attempt more passive approaches to control you, but the balance of power has now shifted out of their hands.

Your situation with an abusive partner might feel more serious, however. It might seem more dangerous or threatening. Maybe your partner controls all the finances, hides the keys to your car, intimates he'll take the kids away or leave you destitute, or spreads false rumors about you. You might feel that if you push back even slightly, you'll lose the crumbs of freedom, affection, money, or social life you have now. His or her emotionally abusive power seems impenetrable.

But even in these cases, your perceptions don't reflect reality. You DO have more power and more options than you think. You may need to engage an attorney, get a counselor involved, or seek help from friends and family before this manipulator backs down and releases control over your life.

You may need to make short-term sacrifices, take some difficult actions, or suffer the embarrassment of revealing your abusive relationship to other people to initiate change. But these sacrifices and discomforts are small compared to a lifetime of mental health problems, unhappiness, and insecurity. Please don't allow your "what if" fears to blind you to the truth of your situation and your own power to take action.

Recently an emotional abuse victim emailed me that she couldn't do anything about her situation because her husband controlled all the money. I suggested she ask to borrow money from her family or friends, and she emailed back saying that her partner prevented her from communicating with her friends and family. However, she had just emailed me, so she did have a portal to the outside world. She could have emailed friends and family or asked me or someone else to do it for her, but her fear prevented her from seeing that.

You must take one small action to regain control of your life despite your fear and discomfort. Challenge your beliefs that your abusive partner holds all the cards. There are cards you haven't played, and as scary as it might feel, you must take the first step because your abuser certainly won't do anything to help you. Reach out to family. Contact an attorney. Set an appointment with a counselor. Take one step to get support as you begin to break free from your abuser's control and power over you.

One important caveat I must add: If your partner has been physically abusive, broken or thrown things in your home, or has threatened physical violence, then the strategies in this book are NOT for you. Physical abuse (or the threat of it) requires the immediate intervention of law enforcement, and a victim needs to do everything possible to protect herself and her children. Do NOT try to stand up to a physical abuser by yourself. You need support in leaving the situation as quickly as possible. Call 911 or contact the National Domestic Violence Hotline at 1-800-799-SAFE (7233) or for the deaf or hard of hearing, contact 1-800-787-3224 (TTY). This is 24/7 confidential phone support with trained advocates. Your life really could depend on it.

Barrie Davenport

Using These Scripts

The best, first step in reclaiming your power and building your confidence is by speaking up. If you have remained silent during and after abusive episodes, or if you've fallen apart or had emotional outbursts in response, you are further disempowering yourself. Only mature, confident, forceful, but calm language affords the power and confidence you need to reclaim your rightful position as an equal partner.

Maybe you've tried to speak up in the past, only to get shot down, dismissed, or yelled at. It didn't seem to work, so you just stopped doing it. However, your first goal is not to get your abuser to stop his or her behaviors. You can't control how he or she chooses to behave. The main goal is to know that *you* haven't allowed him or her to simply get away with it.

If you want to become more empowered, speaking up can't be an occasional response to the abuse. You must repeat your expectations, frustrations, and feelings about the abuse every single time. Remember, you are speaking up more for yourself

11

and your own dignity than you are to convince your abuser to change.

How your abuser responds to your words over time will give you a great deal of information on how YOU want to proceed in the relationship. It's highly likely your abusive partner won't respond well to your pushback, at least in the beginning. If his or her behavior doesn't change over time, or if your partner refuses counseling, then you have a big decision to make. Do you want to live with this behavior for the rest of your life and try to manage it, or is it time to let go of the relationship and move on? If you want more insight into how to make this decision, please read my book called *Emotional Abuse Breakthrough: How to Speak Up, Set Boundaries, and Break the Cycle of Manipulation and Control with Your Abusive Partner* (See http://liveboldandbloom.com/eab-book).

The purpose of this book is to give you templates for knowing what to say to your abusive partner for as long as you are in the relationship or still dealing with the abuser (as an ex-partner or soon-to-be ex-partner).

The scripts included in this book cover a variety of situations related to emotionally abusive relationships, including responses to some of the more common abusive behaviors. I've also included scripts for telling your abuser you are leaving the relationship, as well as communicating with your children about the end of the relationship.

As you review these scripts, here are some important considerations to remember:

1. Consistency Is Key

As I mentioned earlier, you can't occasionally throw out a comment like, "That's unacceptable language," and have any credibility with your abuser or within yourself. You need to make a commitment to yourself that you will be consistent in calling out the abuse when (or soon after) it occurs, even if it happens in front of other people. You may feel like a broken record, but it's critical that you point out the behavior every single time.

2. Keep Your Expectations Low

More than likely, your abuser will not respond well to this "new you" who is speaking out against his or her behavior. In fact, the abuse may get worse before it gets better. You may get responses that are angry, sarcastic, defensive, or dismissive. You might be taunted with words like, "What are you gonna do about it?"

Your abuser doesn't expect much from you. He or she thinks you'll back down soon enough and doesn't take you seriously. As you begin standing up for yourself and speaking out, expect little change from your abuser. Don't worry if it doesn't seem to be "working." It's working for you, because you are now shifting the balance of power.

3. Establish Boundaries and Consequences

If some situations, you will need to communicate specific boundaries, and if these boundaries are crossed, you'll need to be prepared with consequences that you are willing to implement

13

consistently. As you read through these scripts and come to a situation that resonates with you, make notes about the boundaries you want to establish for the situation and the specific actions you'll take if the boundaries are ignored. (More on this in the next section of the book.)

4. Implement Consequences Every Single Time

Never threaten something you don't intend to follow through on. If you say, "I'm leaving you, if you do that one more time," then be prepared to leave. Otherwise, your abuser has just gained the upper hand. That's why it's important to be prepared with consequences you are willing to implement.

Your abuser is a master of manipulation, so he or she will be relentless in trying to get you to forget your consequences or let it go "this one time." Don't fall for it. The abuser must know you mean business.

5. Never React, Just Respond

The beauty of consequences is the silent power they afford. If your abuser breaks your boundaries or crosses the line, don't cry, whine, cajole, scream, or offer any other emotional reaction. Just act. Implement the consequences as soon as possible. Don't placate your abuser no matter how compelling her "act" might be. Don't fall for guilt trips or excuses.

6. Never Engage in Word Battles

Abusers are masterful at twisting language, pointing the finger of blame, and trying to deflect the conversation away from their own bad behaviors. If you state your case, speak up, or institute a boundary; don't engage in long diatribes about what you have said, how the abuser feels, or what they want instead. Simply say, "That's all I'm going to say on the matter." And then leave the room. Or the house. Do not try to negotiate, be "understanding," or offer a listening ear to a litany of problems and complaints.

7. Give Specifics, Ask for Specifics

Communicate in clear, unambiguous language. For example, say, "If you don't have the money in my account by 3:00 tomorrow, I will call my lawyer to help me handle it through the court system." Don't say something ambiguous like, "I really need the money because it's my money too. You're being unfair. There are laws about this you know."

If you need something from your abuser, ask for it specifically and continue to ask until you get a specific answer. "I need an exact date and time this week that you will join me for a counseling session." If the response is, "I don't know. I'm not sure yet," then go back to the question or say, "At what point today will you know for sure?"

8. Think Ahead and Practice

You know the most common scenarios of abuse in your relationship. You know what hurts, controls, or offends you the most. Think about how these situations unfold, what triggers them, and what you and your abuser generally say and do. Find a script (or write your own based on these) that works for the situation, and practice saying it out loud. Use a firm, clear voice and make eye contact. Even if your knees are shaking, act as though you feel in command and confident. The more you practice, the more easily the words will come to you in a heated situation.

9. Consider Timing

There are situations in which it's better to address the abusive actions or words after the fact rather than during the event. For example, if your abuser is angry and yelling, and your kids are in the room, it may be better to say, "Let's discuss this when things calm down," rather than, "You are being verbally abusive, and I won't put up with it." This might escalate things in front of your kids. Wait until it's just you and your partner so you don't further upset your children.

10. Solicit Support

You may want to review your intended responses and scripts with a counselor or trusted friend. Every emotionally abusive relationship is different, and your life circumstances may require responses tailored to what you can reasonably manage within these circumstances. There isn't a one-size-fits-all response for all abusive scenarios.

Talk with someone about the boundaries you want to set, the consequences you can realistically enforce, and the outcomes you hope to achieve in the short term. Practice your scripts with this person so he or she can give you feedback and help you feel more empowered and confident as you speak them.

Barrie Davenport

A Word about Boundaries and Consequences

If you are just beginning to stand up to your partner about his or her emotional abuse and to speak out against it, please don't expect a positive reaction right away. As I mentioned earlier, the abuse may get worse before it gets better. You may have to repeat your feelings and boundaries many times before your partner realizes you are serious.

It's important that you clearly state your boundaries repeatedly about what you do and do not find acceptable in your relationship. As you read through the scripts that follow, you'll see I've included boundary statements related to each particular offense. When your boundaries are honored by your partner without the need for consequences, be sure to offer positive reinforcement and appreciation.

However, words only go so far, and eventually they must be reinforced with logical consequences. A consequence is either removing the desirable or adding the undesirable to your partner's life as the result of crossing a boundary and repeating abusive behaviors.

Evaluate how chronic, destructive, and severe the boundary violation is. Depending on the severity of the offense, you may be willing to give two or three warnings before you implement a consequence. And you want to give the most lenient consequence that works. For example, if your partner uses sarcasm with you, it might be extreme to say, "I'm leaving you the next time that happens." But if your partner screams and curses at you, and has been doing it for years, then a serious consequence is merited.

It's important to think ahead about consequences that are appropriate for the offense, as well as when you are willing to implement them, how many chances you will offer, and whether or not you intend to follow through if the boundary is crossed. But remember, it's better to hold off on announcing a consequence if you don't have the strength to follow through. Start with small consequences that reinforce your independence but that aren't life-changing.

Consequences are not retribution or punishment. They are logical, appropriate actions that force your abuser to make a more conscious choice about his behavior and that reflect your new state of mind and inner strength. They are about allowing realistic cause and effect so that your spouse will experience the pain of irresponsibility and then hopefully change.

Here's a list of possible consequences you can think about as you review the scripts:
- Saying no or refusing a request.
- Refusing to reply until the abuser is calm.

- Ending a conversation.
- Leaving the room.
- Leaving the house for a short time.
- Leaving a restaurant, party, or another public place.
- Calling out the abuser's bad behavior in front of others.
- Refusing to participate in or attend an event.
- Sleeping in a separate room.
- Ending sexual contact until an issue is discussed or resolved maturely.
- Hiring a housekeeper, lawn care person, cook, or babysitter if partner doesn't help.
- Leaving for a few days to stay with friends or family.
- Going on "strike" (from housekeeping, preparing meals, chores) until the abuser steps up.
- Talking with friends or family members about the abuse.
- Going to a counselor on your own to talk about the abuse.
- Meeting with an attorney to discuss your options.
- Meeting with a financial advisor to discuss your options.
- Getting your own job or changing jobs.
- Filing for a legal separation.
- Moving out of the house.
- Filing a restraining order.
- Filing for divorce.
- Moving to another state.

As you read through the scripts below, make notes about the boundaries you want to establish and the consequences you can realistically enforce. Remember, a consequence must matter to your partner, and he or she must be emotionally invested in it. Otherwise, the experience doesn't count for much. When you announce a consequence, follow through on it as quickly as possible. This is as important for your own self-esteem as it is for changing your abuser's behavior.

Scripts for a General Wake-Up Call for the Abuser

In my book, *Emotional Abuse Breakthrough*, I discuss the point you may reach in which you make a firm decision that you no longer intend to accept your partner's abuse. You recognize the abuse for what it is and how your partner is denying you the kind of loving, respectful relationship you deserve.

When you reach this point, it's important to have an initial conversation with your partner to let him know that things are about to shift. This isn't an easy conversation to have, especially if you aren't accustomed to being proactive this way, or you fear your partner will get angry or cause a scene.

Try to keep this initial conversation short, to the point, and free of intense emotion. You are giving your partner a heads-up that things are changing. You'll have plenty of time to address specific behaviors as time goes on.

If your partner gets angry or defensive immediately, end the conversation, but invite him or her to return to it once things calm down.

Barrie Davenport

Script #1: We Need Counseling

The way you've been treating me is not the way a loving partner (spouse) should behave. I've been reading about relationship problems, and your behavior and words are emotionally abusive. I can no longer accept being treated this way. We need counseling if this relationship is going to survive.

Script #2: Calling Out the Abuse

What you are saying (or doing) is unloving, unkind, and manipulative. I will not accept it. I am leaving the room, and we can discuss this when you are able to speak (or behave) kindly.

Script #3: Announcing You Have Changed

I want you to know that I have changed. I can no longer accept the way you treat me and the kind of relationship we have. We need counseling right away, if our relationship is going to make it. I have set an appointment for next Tuesday. Are you in?

Script #4: Demanding Equal Partnership

I know I've allowed you to make all the decisions and manage everything in our lives, but I'm learning that's not the way a real relationship works. I want things to change because I am changing. I want an equal partnership with someone who treats me with kindness, love, and respect. Can you step up to that?

Script #5: Stating Your Feelings

I am extremely unhappy with our marriage (relationship). I do not like the way you are treating me and speaking to me. I don't like the way you try to manipulate and control me by raising your voice or trying to make me feel guilty. I want a loving, healthy relationship, but this isn't it. We need help to get our marriage back on track. Do you want that too?

Script #6: Pointing Out Behavior

This is the exact behavior I've been talking to you about—exactly what you are doing right now. I don't like it and will not put up with it any longer. Either stop now, or I'm leaving the house. It is unacceptable to me.

Barrie Davenport

Scripts for Dominating and Controlling Words and Behaviors

Control and domination are a big part of the abuser's arsenal. They use intimidation and passive-aggressive behaviors to force you to toe the line. Sometimes this control is subtle, like giving you a nasty look, but other times it is more overt and frightening, like cursing and yelling at you.

When you call out your abuser on these behaviors, and you don't respond or react to them by cowering, acquiescing, or getting angry yourself, you are sending a powerful message to your abuser that you are much stronger and more in control than he or she anticipated.

Script #7: Making Faces and Giving Looks

When you roll your eyes and look bored while I'm talking, it tells me you don't respect me. It's demeaning and unkind. Do you want to be demeaning and unkind? If not, then please stop doing that. If you do, then we have a problem and need counseling.

27

Script #8: Talking Down to You

You are speaking to me like I'm a child. I'm not a child. I'm your partner. I want you to stop trying to control and talk down to me. I want you to speak to me kindly and with respect because that's what I deserve, and it's the way a loving spouse should speak.

Script #9: Giving Nasty Looks

I can see by your expression that you don't like what I said (or think I'm wrong). Giving me nasty looks is unkind and tells me you don't respect me. If you need to tell me something, you can communicate with calm, productive words.

Script #10: Controlling Your Activities

I am going to spend time with my friends and family, and I don't need your permission to do so. I'll let you know where I'm going and when I'll be back so you don't worry, but if you keep calling and checking up on me, I will no longer respond. It is controlling and demeaning when you monitor what I do all the time. Please stop it.

Script #11: Monitoring Your Calls and Texts

I do not like it when you look at my phone calls and texts. If you don't trust me, then we can discuss your feelings and reasons for not trusting me. But I have put a password on my phone and won't be sharing it. I am allowed some privacy in my life.

Script #12: Controlling Your Decisions

You make me feel like a prisoner in my own home, and this has got to stop. You can't continue to control my life and decisions. I am your partner, not a child. Starting today things have to change. Here's what I plan to do.

Script #13: Controlling the Money

We are a couple, and the money we have is ours together. It is as much my decision how it is spent as yours, and I should have equal access to it. Let's go over our finances and decide how we manage our money and what we each can use for discretionary spending. I want to have a new system starting today.

Script #14: Shutting You Out of Financial Decisions

When you shut me out of financial decisions and put me on a budget, you are treating me like a child. I am your spouse, not a child. By law, I have equal rights to our money. Please don't put me in the position of getting the legal system involved. We need to make some changes starting today.

Script #15: Controlling Family Decisions

In the past, I didn't speak up when you made big decisions for our family without my support or knowledge, even if I disagreed with them. But that is changing today. We are a team, and I am your partner. If there is a decision that affects both of us (or our family), we need to make it together From now on, please don't take action or make decisions without discussing it with me, so we can come to a mutual agreement.

Scripts for Verbal Abuse

Verbal abuse can be overtly threatening, frightening, and openly cruel. This kind of verbal abuse involves yelling, cursing, name-calling, bullying, and suggestions of future physical violence.

However, many verbal abusers aren't as direct or threatening. Instead, they twist language and words so the recipients aren't really sure what's hit them. They use a subtle form of verbal abuse that is so convoluted and disconcerting that it's difficult to call it out and take action. Because it can't be clearly defined, you may believe you're imagining it or even the cause of it.

Over time, you begin to recognize the subtler forms of verbal abuse for what they are. You know your partner is trying to make you feel bad, control you, or manipulate your behavior. Whether it's openly aggressive or more covert, verbal abuse is tremendously damaging to your self-esteem.

Script #16: Raising Voice and Cursing

I see that you're trying to upset and frighten me with your raised voice and cursing. In the past, it did make me feel afraid, but not any more. If you raise your voice and curse again, I'll leave the room until you can talk calmly. I'm not putting up with it any longer.

Script #17: Using Sarcasm

I do not like the sarcasm you are using. It isn't funny, and it's not teasing. It is hurtful and unloving. I want you to stop using it from now on. I want you to speak to me kindly and respectfully, and if you can't, I will end the conversation until you can.

Script #18: Insulting and Demeaning You

Stop insulting me right now. That is unacceptable. I am your spouse, the person you love, and your language is totally demeaning and hurtful. I will not stand for it.

Script #19: Raising His or Her Voice

You do not need to raise your voice. I can hear you perfectly well when you speak calmly. If you can't talk to me calmly, then we need to discuss this later when you can.

Script #20: Mimicking and Insulting You

If you insist on mimicking me and insulting me, then I'll need to leave until you can speak to me respectfully. I want healthy, adult communication from now on, or I will end the conversation.

Script #21: Using Profanity

You do not have to use profanity to make your point. I am no longer willing to endure your onslaught of profanity whenever you don't like something. Either speak to me calmly without cursing, or I will end the conversation.

Barrie Davenport

Scripts for Demanding Expectations

Emotional abusers have little respect for your time and life priorities. They expect you to jump when they say jump, and they don't mind inconveniencing you in the process. This narcissistic behavior reveals a lack of real care and concern about your needs and feelings.

Some abusers believe they are the king or queen of the household, as though they don't have an obligation or responsibility to tend to housework, childcare, or other tasks they find beneath them or simply don't want to deal with. They either demand you take care of it or passively leave it in your hands by refusing to participate.

If you express your own opinions, desires, needs, or feelings, many emotional abusers will feel threatened and demand that you keep your thoughts to yourself. They may expect you to fall in line related to childrearing, political views, religion, and your feelings about friends and family.

Script #22: Interrupting or Demanding Your Attention

I am happy to talk to you, but not when you interrupt me or demand my attention when I'm clearly doing something else. When I finish what I'm doing, we can have this conversation.

Script #23: Ordering You Around

Please stop ordering me around. I am your partner, not your servant or child. If you want something, ask me politely.

Script #24: Expecting You to Agree on Everything

Because I disagree with you doesn't mean I am being disrespectful. I have my own opinions, and sometimes they are different from yours. I am my own person, and you need to accept that without getting angry or defensive.

Script #25: Unequal Share of Childcare and Housework

As partners, we are equally responsible for taking care of the housework and children when we are both at home. It is unfair and selfish for you to expect me to handle everything. I have made a list of how we can divide responsibilities, and I'd like to discuss it. If we can't agree to something, we need a counselor to help us figure it out.

Script #26: Demanding Expectations

Your expectations of me are unreasonable and demanding. This is not a dictatorship; it's a partnership. I am happy to have a calm discussion about a request, but I will no longer jump to your demands or respond to angry complaints. You will have to take care of (dinner, laundry, paying bills, cleaning the garage, etc.) yourself if you continue treating me like a servant.

Script #27: Not Participating with Kids

You are the father (or mother) of our children. It's not only your responsibility to share in taking care of them, but they need your participation. They need to see you care enough to be fully involved in parenting them. I want to talk about how to share childcare between us more fairly.

Script #28: Refusing to Clean Up

When you refuse to clean up after yourself or help in cleaning the house, it makes me feel like a servant. We live here together, and I'm not a servant, I'm your partner. You need to respect me enough to clean up after yourself and share in keeping the house clean. I will not be cleaning up after you any longer.

Barrie Davenport

Scripts for Emotional Blackmail

Emotional blackmail is the go-to tactic used by abusers to get their own way. Your abuser might suggest you do something unreasonable or act against your values or desires. If you don't comply, he uses subtle emotional threats to strong-arm and intimidate you until you do.

He might try to embarrass you into compliance by raising his voice in front of guests or out at dinner, knowing you don't want others to see you fighting. She might act like a martyr or attempt to shame you into taking a desired action or giving in to a whim.

Your abuser might try to blame you for her unhappiness or for a problem between you so that you feel guilty and acquiesce to her demands. You might get the cold shoulder or denial of sex to punish you until you give in. Maybe she leaves the house for hours when you don't comply, or she implies she's going to divorce you unless you give in.

All of these tactics are manipulative, selfish, and uncaring, and you shouldn't accept them as a "normal" response to relationship conflict. Intimidation and subtle threats have no place in a loving, healthy relationship.

Script #29: Yelling to Keep You Quiet

I see that you are trying to keep me quiet by yelling at me when I disagree with you. That used to work, but not any longer. I will state my feelings and thoughts whether or not you choose to raise your voice. But I will not listen to you or respond to your comments when you yell at me.

Script #30: Using Guilt Trips to Control

Trying to make me feel guilty will no longer work with me. Guilt trips are manipulative and demeaning, and I won't fall for them any more. If you are unhappy or frustrated, let's have an adult conversation, but no more guilt trips.

Script #31: Using Shame to Control

I see that you are trying to shame me into doing what you want. You are trying to control my behavior by making me feel bad about myself. That is hurtful and manipulative, and I won't tolerate it any longer. If you continue, I will end the conversation.

Script #32: Using Sex as a Weapon

It's clear that you are using sex as a weapon to punish me or send me a message. That is manipulative and pushes us further apart. If you want us to be close, you need to have a calm conversation with me about what's on your mind rather than using sex against me.

Script #33: Being Cold and Distant

You are being cold and emotionally distant with me, and it is hurtful. But I'm not going to do backflips to try to win your love and affection. I'm happy to talk with you calmly about anything that's bothering you, but your coldness is pushing me away from you. Is that what you want? If not, then let's talk and work on being close again.

Script #34: Disappearing after an Argument

When you slam out of the house and disappear after an argument, it used to make me feel afraid and abandoned. But now I know you are doing it for that reason, so I'll give in and do what you want. I'm not going to tolerate that any longer. If you storm out of the house and leave me wondering where you are and when you'll be back, then I will need to go stay with a friend until you can handle disagreements more calmly and maturely.

Script #35: Threatening to Leave

I want you to stop threatening to leave me unless you really mean it. Those words have become meaningless to me. If you really want to leave, let's talk about the next steps.

Script #36: Not Caring about Your Feelings

I have told you many times how much that hurts me (offends me, embarrasses me, etc.), but you continue to do it. It is clear that my feelings are not important to you. In a loving marriage, both of us should respect and honor each other's feelings. Are you committed to making this marriage work?

Scripts for Unpredictable Behavior

That anxious feeling of walking on eggshells is so common in emotionally abusive relationships because the abuser's behavior is so unpredictable. One minute your partner is the kind, loving, happy person you fell in love with. But without warning, he transforms from Dr. Jekyll into Mr. Hyde.

Something has set him off, and he's in your face, yelling and cursing at you, his face twisted in anger. Or she becomes frustrated by some minor incident and suddenly starts slamming doors and banging pots around in the kitchen to get your attention.

This unpredictable behavior can take many forms, as your abuser knows exactly what to do to keep you off-balance. He or she might drive recklessly while you're in the car to scare you. She might suddenly go completely silent or berate you loudly in a public place.

Even though this behavior is disconcerting and even scary, you shouldn't put up with it. It is a childish, selfish attempt to gain the upper hand and keep you in a state of confusion and fear.

Script #37: Emotional Outbursts

I know you are using these emotional outbursts to get my attention and force me to do what you want. But I'm not falling for it any longer. You can continue this tantrum, or we can talk like two mature adults. Your choice.

Script #38: Stomping Out of the Room

Stomping out of the room every time we have a disagreement is not productive or healthy for our connection. It makes it impossible to have a real discussion, and it shuts things down completely. We can't solve anything if you do this. Are you willing to stop it?

Script #39: Sulking and Silent Treatment

I know you want to punish me by sulking and giving the silent treatment, but this behavior only damages our relationship and intimacy. I want you to stop this behavior now and have an adult conversation about what's going on.

Script #40: Intimidating Faces and Finger Pointing

I want you to stop getting in my face and shaking your finger at me. Back off right now. That is totally unacceptable. This conversation has ended until you calm down.

Scripts for Chaos and Crisis Creation

Many emotional abusers enjoy or find satisfaction in creating drama and chaos. In the same way they attempt to keep you off-balance with unpredictable behavior, they will look for ways to stir the pot to control you.

When life is calm and happy, you might feel empowered to speak up for yourself, make your own choices, or assume your partner has finally seen the light and will treat you as an equal. As you know, this peaceful state is short-lived. Soon enough, something crazy and dramatic happens to pull the rug out from under you.

She might try to bait you into an argument by making unkind or challenging remarks. His jealously about your friendships might flare up, and he yells at your friends to leave the house.

Your spouse might constantly find something wrong with your family and create a drama or pout when they are around. He might intentionally do something that he knows will make you uncomfortable, like cursing in public or yelling at a waiter. She might drink too much and act ridiculous or make a scene, despite you asking her not to have another drink.

Creating drama and chaos provides the abusers the upper hand because they can tolerate (or even enjoy) it while you feel embarrassed, uncomfortable, and ashamed. Your abuser knows you'll do just about anything to regain "normalcy," and he or she takes full advantage of that.

Script #41: Unwarranted Jealous Behavior

Your unwarranted jealousy of my friends is tearing us apart. Your behavior toward them and me is embarrassing and unkind. If you can't stop this on your own, you need to work with a counselor to manage your jealous feelings.

Script #42: Crossing Your Boundaries

I have asked you many times to stop grabbing my butt in public (or crossing some other boundary). I don't like it, and I won't put up with it. You are not respecting me, and it's selfish and unkind.

Script #43: Blaming You for His or Her Unhappiness

I am not to blame for your unhappiness (failure, frustration, etc.). I want you to stop blaming me right now. You are an adult and need to take responsibility for your life. I love you and will support you, but I will not take the blame.

Script #44: Trying to Spite You

It is clear you did that (or said that) just to spite me. That is deeply hurtful and unkind. You are not behaving the way a loving spouse should behave by trying to get back at me, and it is severely damaging our relationship.

Script #45: Baiting You to Argue

I know you are trying to engage me in an argument, and in the past I would have taken the bait. But I won't fall for it any longer. I'm happy to have a real conversation, but I'm not going to argue with you, plain and simple.

Script #46: Compulsive Lying

Your compulsive lying is obvious to me and everyone close to you. I know you aren't being truthful, and it is eroding my trust and respect for you. If our relationship will work, you must practice being truthful 100 percent of the time.

Barrie Davenport

Scripts for Character Assassination

Emotional abusers show little respect for their partners, and nothing makes this clearer than the way they put you down and insult you. To build themselves up, shore up their own self-esteem, and keep you under control, they will call you names, make fun of you, treat you like a child, and withhold praise.

Rather than focusing on your positive qualities, which are generally ignored, your abuser only seems to notice your flaws and feels no reticence about pointing them out. They feel free to "correct" your behavior and chastise you, even in front of other people, in an attempt to diminish your intelligence or capability.

Your abuser might laugh at you, act condescending, or suggest you're being too sensitive or irrational. All these tactics slowly strip away your self-esteem and faith in your own judgment and abilities. If your own spouse thinks you're a loser, you must be pretty bad.

The truth is, it's your abusive partner's character that is flawed. Loving, mature, supportive partners would never intentionally insult or shame the person they love most. This is cruel, hurtful behavior that kills any intimacy and connection you have with this person. How can real love exist in this toxic environment?

Script #47: Put-Downs in Front of Others

It is humiliating and hurtful when you put me down in front of my friends. I will not take it any longer. If it happens again, I am going to call you out on it and leave the room.

Script #48: Making Fun of You

This is a perfect example of how you make fun of my appearance (intellect, education, etc.). That is just plain mean and hurtful. I want you to stop doing that right now. It is unacceptable, and I won't stand for it.

Script #49: Chastising and Correcting You

I am not a child, and you don't need to chastise me or correct my behavior. I want you to stop doing that right now. If you have a problem with something I'm doing, we can discuss it like adults.

Script #50: Refusing to Offer Praise and Support

I want you to be proud of me and my accomplishments, but it's clear you have a hard time offering me praise and supporting my dreams.

Are you able to step up and do that for me? If not, I'd rather you say nothing than offer watered-down comments or criticisms.

Script #51: Pointing Out Your Flaws

I know I have flaws and I'm not perfect. But neither are you. I want you to stop pointing out my flaws and criticizing me all the time. We need to have each other's backs, not tear each other down. Are you in?

Script #52: Betraying Your Confidences

When I tell you things in confidence, it is a huge betrayal when you share them with your friends. We are partners, and you should be the person I can trust the most. We can't have real intimacy without that trust between us.

Script #53: Telling You Your Feelings Are Irrational

I want you to stop telling me my feelings are wrong or I'm irrational. My feelings are my feelings, and as my spouse you should treat them with dignity, not try to undermine them. Can you respect me enough to do that?

Script #54: Putting Down Your Family and Friends

You may not like my mom (or friend, sister, etc.), but I care about her deeply, so when you put her down, it's also putting me down. I'm happy to discuss a specific problem you have with her, but these constant negative remarks must stop. I won't tolerate them any more.

Scripts for Gaslighting

Gaslighting is a term that originates from a 1944 movie called *Gaslight* in which the husband subtly tries to make his wife doubt her perceptions.

When your partner gaslights you, he or she might deny something that you both know is true or pretend something happened that really didn't. She might suggest you're lying or exaggerating in an attempt to make you feel stupid or crazy. This is a way to control you and to allow your partner to shirk responsibility for his or her actions.

Your abuser might play mind games with you to see your reaction and gauge how much actual control she has over you, or to test her beliefs and insecurities in the relationship. She might try to confuse a serious conversation by diverting it away from your main issue or concern. He might try to deflect blame to you for something that is clearly his fault.

One form of gaslighting that you will more than likely encounter is a denial from your abuser that he or she is emotionally abusing you. Your abuser may pretend he doesn't know what you're talking about, even when you are clear and offer specific examples and incidences of the abuse.

Gaslighting is a particularly insidious, calculating form of emotional abuse that reflects the abuser's callous feelings toward you and your emotional well-being. Loving, supportive partners would never want to manipulate and confuse you intentionally and watch you suffer, knowing they are playing games with you.

Script #55: Accusing You of Being Too Sensitive

No, I'm not "too sensitive." You are being deliberately thoughtless and unkind. Do you care that your remarks are hurting and offending me? If so, you need to change them starting today.

Script #56: Trying to Confuse the Situation

You are not being straight with me, and it's clear you're trying to confuse the situation at hand so I doubt myself. I'm not falling for it. I know exactly what you're doing, and I won't put it with it any longer.

Script #57: Playing Mind Games with You

Don't try to play mind games with me. I know exactly what you're up to, and I won't be intimidated. If this relationship is going to work, you need to be up front and have real, honest communication with me.

Script #58: Deflecting the Blame to You

This mistake (problem, failure) is yours and yours alone. Don't try to blame me for it. I will help and support you, but I'm not falling for finger pointing and excuses. You made the choices that led to this situation.

Script #59: Making Untrue Allegations

I am not going to continue to defend myself against unwarranted and untrue accusations. A relationship must be based on trust, and I've given you no reason to mistrust me. Stop blaming me for things we both know are not true. You are harming our relationship severely when you do this.

Script #60: Denying the Emotional Abuse

When you deny that your words and behaviors are emotionally abusive, it tells me you aren't really invested in the health of our relationship. It also tells me you don't value my feelings and concerns. This is a serious problem for me, and you should take it seriously if you want things to work between us.

Barrie Davenport

Scripts for Sexual Harassment and Abuse

Does your partner try to force you through words or actions to engage in sexual activity against your will? Does he force himself on you, even when you say "No"? If so, this is a form of harassment and abuse.

If your partner tries to make you (through physical force, threats, insults, guilt trips, etc.) engage in sexual acts that you don't feel comfortable with, this is also sexual harassment and abuse. If any sexual advances are unwanted, and you make it known that they are unwanted and want it to stop, but he or she continues, then its harassment.

Some abusers assume they have sexual "rights" to their partner, whether or not the partner agrees to the sexual encounter. The abuser cajoles, guilt-trips, shames, or does whatever it takes to coerce or force the victim into sexual activity. This sometimes includes forced sex.

In fact, until 1975, every state in the United States had a "marital exemption" that allowed a husband to rape his wife without fear of legal consequences.

Since 1993, all 50 states have enacted laws against marital rape, but, even so, it is still difficult to prove spousal rape.

Please note that spousal or intimate partner rape is a form of physical violence that goes beyond just manipulation and psychological coercion. If sexual harassment has turned into forced sexual acts, please contact the National Domestic Abuse Hotline, law enforcement, or your counselor to get the support you need.

Using sex to manipulate, control, embarrass, or shame the person who is supposed to be your most intimate partner is the ultimate act of selfishness and disrespect. It can be one of the most damaging forms of emotional (and physical) abuse.

Script #61: Pressuring You to Have Sex

I want you to stop harassing me to have sex. For sex to be enjoyable for me, we need to be in a loving and kind space together. Pressuring and shaming makes me want to avoid sex altogether. When you treat me with love, kindness, and respect, that's when I want to have sex with you.

Script #62: Crossing Your Sexual Boundaries

I do not feel comfortable doing that, and I never will. Stop trying to force me or cajole me into doing it now and forever. Respect my boundaries so that we can have a good sex life, or we'll need to go to counseling to figure it out.

Script #63: Demeaning You during Sex

You may not demean me or make insulting comments about my body during sex. That is deeply unkind and hurtful, and I won't stand for it. I cannot be intimate with someone who speaks this way to me.

Script #64: Threatening to Cheat on You

Stop threatening to cheat on me when I don't feel like having sex. I am not available to you every moment you want sex. I'm your partner, not just a sexual outlet for you. If you need more sex, we can go to counseling to talk about how to improve our sex life. But threatening affairs will only make things worse between us.

Barrie Davenport

.

Scripts for Abuser Emotionally Abusing Your Kids

If you have children at home, you have another compelling reason to take a stand against the abuse your partner inflicts on you and on them. You need to protect your children from witnessing abusive behaviors toward you or between you and your partner.

Simply being in an abusive environment is a form of emotional abuse for your children. Witnessing a parent being berated, insulted, ignored, shamed, or threatened by another parent is deeply disturbing and confusing for children who have no way of comprehending what's happening or how to manage their feelings about it.

It is also critically important to prevent your children from being crushed by emotionally abusive words and behaviors inflicted on them by the abuser. They must have at least one parent who will stand up for them and protect them from the emotional damage of this kind of abuse.

Your partner may exhibit his abusive behaviors with your children for the same reasons he or she abuses you. If he constantly criticizes, berates, belittles, teases, or frightens your child, this is abuse and must be stopped, and you must be the one to stop it. There is no one else in the home who can protect your children from the lifelong pain of emotional abuse.

Once you take a stand for what you will no longer accept, you also need to take a stand for your children. There is a big difference between loving and appropriate discipline and severe and unjust punishment, manipulation, and control. If you are anxious and fearful around your abuser, you can only imagine how your children must feel.

Script #65: Yelling at Your Children

Your constant yelling at our son is frightening him, and it's abusive. He can't defend himself against your anger. You need to stop treating him this way right now. I won't allow it.

Script #66: Undermining You with Children

We need to have a united front in parenting our kids. When you undermine my authority with them, you are creating confusion and internal conflict for them that they can't manage. I want you to stop doing this and have a conversation with me so we can decide together the consequences for the kids.

Script #67: Using Guilt Trips and Sarcasm with Children

You may not be aware of it, but you are using guilt trips and sarcasm with our children. They are too young and too suggestible to know how to handle this. You need to stop doing it right now.

Script #68: Frightening the Kids by Abusing You

When you yell and curse at me, the kids hear everything. It's not only abusive to me, but it's abusive to them. You need to stop it right now. You are damaging them with this behavior.

Script #69: Shaming Your Children

You are using shaming, hurtful words with Steven, and it is emotionally abusive. I won't tolerate you treating our child this way. You must stop this immediately.

Script #70: Withholding Affection from Your Children

Nicole feels rejected and unloved by you when you push her away and don't give her affection. You are not giving her the love and attention she needs as your child, and that is neglectful and cruel. You need to step up and parent her with the love she deserves.

Script #71: Making Your Children Confidants

Michael is a child, not an adult. He can't deal with your problems, and he can't be your confidant. You are burdening him with information he isn't able to cope with. Stop doing that, and find an adult you can talk with, if you can't talk with me.

Scripts for Last Chance with the Abuser

Unfortunately, most emotional abusers don't give up their bad behaviors voluntarily. For an abuser to change, he or she must accept full responsibility and acknowledge that abuse is a choice. Your partner must accept that overcoming his or her abusive behavior and attitudes can take decades and not proclaim they are "cured" after a counseling session or two.

In addition, if your partner is truly motivated to recover, he or she must develop respectful, kind, supportive behaviors with you and your children, and change how they respond to your pain, anger, and frustrations.

If your spouse has shown a real interest in changing and is willing to go to counseling and work on his or her issues, there is hope for your relationship. However, you may be required to draw a line in the sand to make it clear to your partner that you truly mean business.

It is particularly important at this point in your relationship that you follow through on your consequences. If this is indeed your partner's last chance to change, then don't give him or her yet another chance.

You may discover that by the time you are willing to draw a line in the sand, you are far past the point of wanting to reconcile. If this is the case, be honest with yourself and your partner. These "last chance" scripts are useful if you think you want to save your marriage or relationship, but your partner hasn't stepped up and made enough change in his or her behaviors.

Sometimes it takes losing someone, or the threat of it, to make an abuser wake up and realize how serious the situation is.

Script #72: Abuser Must Go to Counseling

I have told you many times how hurtful and damaging your emotionally abusive behavior and words are to me. I have asked you to change, and I've given you many chances. Now I'm drawing a line in the sand. If you don't go to counseling for a year to work on changing your behaviors, this marriage is over. I will seek a divorce. What do you choose?

Script #73: Last Chance with Counseling

On Friday at 3:00, you and I have an appointment with a marriage counselor. If you don't go and continue to go to work on our marriage, I will leave the marriage. Will you be joining me?

Script #74: Leaving If Abuse Happens Again

The next time you say that (or do that) to me will be the last time. If it happens again, I'm leaving you.

Script #75: Last Chance with Counseling

I love you, and I want our relationship to work, but not the way it's working right now. You need to make some serious changes in your behavior and how you treat me. I will no longer stand for your controlling, abusive behavior. If you agree to go to counseling right away, I'll give us another chance. If not, then I'm done.

Script #76: Need a Separation with Counseling

I am emotionally exhausted and at the end of my rope. If you want this relationship to continue, I need us to separate while you get counseling. You need to move out and work on changing your abusive behaviors. We can reevaluate things in six months.

Script #77: Acknowledge the Abuse or It's Over

You have a choice. You can either acknowledge your emotionally abusive behaviors and start changing them, or we end this relationship right now. What do you choose? Not making a choice is telling me it's over.

Barrie Davenport

Scripts for Ending Your Relationship with the Abuser

The time will come when you have enough information to help you make the decision to leave the marriage or relationship. After all the evidence is in, after counseling (or attempts at counseling), after working on yourself, taking a stand with your partner, and keeping your children's well-being in mind, you have made the choice to end it.

If you've been intimidated or fearful of your spouse or partner throughout the relationship, the thought of telling him or her that you are leaving is enough to make you want to pass out. How will they react? What will they do to you or your family? Can you handle their response and the subsequent fallout?

In my book, *Emotional Abuse Breakthrough,* I detail all the practical actions and precautions you might take as you prepare to end the relationship. Thoughtful preparation, planning, and consultation with a counselor and an attorney will make the actual moment of telling your abuser much less daunting.

It's also helpful to try to anticipate how your partner will react to your news. You've lived with this person long enough to know his or her patterns of behaviors and typical reactions to information they find negative. Before blurting out your news in a moment of anger or anxiety, think about the best way and place to break it to them.

You may want to do it in a counselor's office, at home with a family member or friend in the house, or even by phone, if you fear your partner's reactions will be unpredictable and frightening.

All the tactics your abuser has used during the relationship will likely get thrown against the wall to see what sticks once you announce your plans. Prepare yourself for these tactics and expect them. You can better prepare yourself by having a few strategies for dealing with your abuser's behavior once you announce you are ending the relationship.

In the moment of breaking the news, try to make your statement clear, concise, and firm, and no matter how your partner reacts, don't engage in an argument or drawn-out conversation. If your decision is final, state your case, give the essential details and information, and then end the conversation. You've likely had dozens (or hundreds) of conversations leading to this moment. You don't need to defend, explain, or apologize.

Script #78: Firm Decision to Divorce

It is clear that things are not improving between us. I can no longer take the control and manipulation or accept your constant criticisms. I have made the decision to get a divorce, and my decision is firm. These are the steps that I've taken so far.

Script #79: Met with an Attorney

For my own mental health, I am ending this relationship. I have thought it over carefully and sought support from a counselor, and this is my firm decision. You have been emotionally abusing me, and you are not serious about changing. I have met with an attorney, and here's what we have put together as a temporary separation agreement until the divorce is final.

Script #80: Calling to End the Relationship

I'm calling from a friend's house to let you know that I've left. I can no longer put up with your abusive words and behaviors. I have taken my personal belongings and have contacted an attorney to file for divorce. My attorney will be contacting you, so please do not contact me directly. You will be receiving more information from him in a few days.

Script #81: Putting the Kids First

Our constant fighting and your abusive behaviors have made it impossible for me to continue with this marriage. It's also taking a huge toll on the kids. I have decided to file for divorce. In the meantime, I hope we can put the kids first while we still live in the same house and create a calm atmosphere for them. If you need to discuss this with me more, we need to do it in a counselor's office. That is the only place I will have a conversation about how to move forward.

Script #82: Stop Harassing So I'll Stay

If you continue to harass me or try to guilt me into staying, I'll have to end all conversation with you. We will have to get a temporary separation agreement that involves one of us moving out. My decision is firm, and you will have to accept it.

Script #83: Announcing Divorce with a Support Person

I've asked my dad (brother, friend, therapist) to be here with me today, because I have something difficult to say, and I want him here to help support me through this discussion. I've made a firm decision to end our relationship and seek a divorce. I will no longer tolerate your emotionally abusive behavior. I have talked with an attorney, and here are my next steps.

Script #84: Announcing Divorce with No Contact

I'm calling (writing) to let you know that I am ending our relationship. My decision is final, and I have moved out and have taken my personal items and other things that belong to me. I've contacted an attorney to file for divorce and to sort out dividing our assets and furnishings. For the time being, you'll need to talk with my attorney if you need to reach me. I won't be answering phone messages or emails from you, as I need this time to figure things out. Here's how you can reach her.

Scripts for Talking with Abuser about Telling the Kids

If it is possible for you and your spouse to talk with your children together about your plans to divorce without criticizing or blaming each other, then this is the best option for a difficult situation.

Ideally, your children should see two mature adults who can calmly discuss this painful decision and accept equal responsibility for the decision to end the marriage (even if this isn't the case). This prevents your children from being in the unnecessary and painful position of choosing sides or looking to blame one of their parents.

If you have initiated the break-up, you will need to ask your partner or spouse to acknowledge that it was a mutual decision or at least be willing to state that it takes two for a marriage to fall apart.

You may have doubts about your partner's ability to step up and protect your children's hearts in this way, so it's important to speak with him or her about it prior to having the discussion with your kids. Hopefully, he or she will see how important it is for your children's innocent psyches to drop the abusive, controlling, or passive-aggressive language long enough to inform your kids.

You might suggest you have the conversation in the presence of a counselor or other helping professional to lessen the chance that your abusive partner will blowup or undermine you in front of the kids. A counselor can also educate you both on the best way to support your children and answer their questions during the transition time before you finalize your divorce.

Script #85: Talk to Kids Together

I'd like us to tell the kids about our divorce together. It is best for their well-being if they feel our decision to divorce is mutual. I hope you will agree to this for their sakes. I have read a lot about the best way to discuss our divorce with the children, and our goal should be to make them feel safe, loved, and not responsible in any way for our problems. They need to feel that neither one of us is at fault so they don't have to choose sides. Can you agree to this? If so, let's discuss exactly what we will say to them and when we will say it.

Script #86: Can Abuser Join Conversation without Anger?

I know you are angry at me about my decision to end our marriage, but we need to create a united front when we tell the children. Are you able to do that? Will you be able to discuss this with them without blaming me, getting angry, or making them feel guilty? If not, then we need to have separate conversations with them or meet with a counselor when we tell them.

Script #87: Telling the Kids with a Counselor

I would like to meet with a counselor along with you and the kids so that we can discuss the divorce and how it will impact them. We are both feeling emotional and raw right now, and a counselor can help us say the best things for the children without anger and blame. I've made an appointment for next week. Will you be there?

Script #88: You've Told the Kids Alone

I want you to know that I have spoken to the children about our plans to divorce. I told them that our marriage is broken and can't be fixed, and that it is no one's fault, especially not theirs. I did not blame you or accuse you of anything. But I couldn't include you in the conversation because of your anger and recent behavior. I hope for their well-being that you will not disparage or blame me when you speak with them. They are far too young to understand what's going on between us. Will you agree to that?

Script #89: Abuser Already Talked to Kids

Since you have already talked to the children about my decision to end our marriage and have blamed me for it, you have put me and them in a difficult position. As a result, I'm taking the kids to a counselor to let them express their concerns and address them in a safe way. I will not blame you, but I will let them know that it takes two people for a marriage to work and two for a marriage to end. Please do not disparage or blame me in front of them again, or you will force me to point this out to the judge in our divorce proceedings.

Scripts for Talking to Your Children about Ending the Relationship

There is no conversation more heart-wrenching than the one in which you must tell your children that you and your spouse are getting divorced. Even if your abuser has been making life miserable for your children as well as for you, your kids will feel deep pain, confusion, and anger at what is happening to their lives and their family.

When you talk with them, there are two critical pieces of information your children need to understand above all else. First, they need to know that they are blameless for the problems between you and your partner that have led to your break-up. Second, they need to know how much they are loved and how your love for them will never end, even though the love between you and your partner hasn't lasted.

In addition, it's important to reassure them that you are OK and that they don't need to worry about you or protect you. They need to see that you are

77

confident and secure, even if you don't feel that way.

An important consideration as you prepare to talk with your children is whether your partner or spouse will be with you as you break the news. Telling them together is the optimal scenario, as it shows your children you are united in your decision (even if you aren't) and that you respect each other and them enough to communicate this difficult news in a mature, loving, adult-like way without undermining or blaming each other.

This may be impossible with an abusive partner who has difficulty with mature communication. He or she may be so angry, hurt, or spiteful that these negative emotions spill out in front of your children, making a painful situation even more difficult and harmful to them.

If you begin the conversation telling your children together, and your partner begins making disparaging remarks or becomes angry, then stop the discussion. Let your children know you'll talk to them again later when things are calmer.

If you suspect this is how your partner may react, or if your spouse has already thrown you under the bus with the children, then having a conversation with your kids by yourself or with your counselor is the best option for your children's mental health and well-being.

Try to keep the conversation calm, loving, and age-appropriate. Children don't need to know all the adult reasons why your marriage or relationship didn't work. Even if your partner criticizes you, try not to reciprocate. Don't put your children in the impossible position to choose sides or figure out the guilty party in the situation.

Script #90: Telling the Kids Together

Dad (or Mom) and I have something important we need to discuss with you, and we are here together so you can ask us both questions. We have decided together that we can no longer be a married couple, and we are getting divorced. But neither of us is leaving you. We will both continue to love you and be here for you as we always have been. Dad and I just can't live together any more because our marriage is broken. It's no one's fault, especially not yours. We know this is sad and scary, and it's OK to cry and feel angry and upset. Do you want to ask us any questions?

Script #91: Telling the Kids with a Counselor

We are having a family meeting with Susan today because she is a counselor, and she's going to help us talk with you about a big decision your mom (or dad) and I have reached. Even though we care about each other very much, we have both reached the decision that we can't live together as a couple any longer. Our marriage isn't working, and it is causing us both too much pain. We know we can be better parents to you and better people if we live apart. No one is to blame, especially not you. We both love you very much, and you had nothing to do with this decision. Susan is going to talk with you a little more and help us answer your questions.

Script #92: Talking to Kids after Abuser Has

I know that Dad (or Mom) has spoken with you about our plans to divorce. I know this was upsetting to you, and I'm so sorry our decision has caused you pain. It is true that I made the final decision to divorce, but our marriage has been broken for a long time, and I was the first person to say it out loud. It takes two people for a marriage to work and two for it to end. I know this is hard for you to understand, but I want you to know that I care for your dad (or mom), and I want you to have a great relationship with him. Nothing will change our love for you, not even our grown-up problems.

Script #93: Responding to Kids Wanting More Information

I know that you want more information about why Dad (or Mom) and I are getting a divorce. But for now, all you need to know is that our marriage wasn't working and could not be fixed, even though Mom says she doesn't want the divorce. I know that's hard for you to understand, and it looks like I'm being mean or hurtful. I'm making the best decisions I can for all of us, even though it doesn't seem that way to you. These are grown-up problems that are personal between me and your mom, and you can't understand them until you are a grown-up yourself. As much as you want more information about our reasons, this is all you need to know. But I can talk to you about your feelings and what the arrangements will be once Mom and I live in different homes.

Script #94: Stopping Discussion when Abuser Gets Angry

Kids, I wanted this conversation to be as calm and honest as possible, and I'm so sorry this is so scary and sad. I think we need to stop the discussion for now until your dad (or mom) feels less angry and upset. What he (she) just said about me isn't the truth and wasn't kind. I'm sorry you had to hear that. Let's go for a walk or go over to Grandma's so we can all take a deep breath and start over with the discussion.

Script #95: Talking to Kids Who Blame You for Divorce

I know that you are angry with me for making the decision to get a divorce. I'm so sorry that you are hurting and that our grown-up problems are causing you so much pain. It is perfectly OK for you to feel angry and sad. I will be here for you, and you can tell me all about how you are feeling, even when you are angry at me. Here is something important for you to know: I hate divorce too, and even though it looks like I made the decision, it takes two people for a marriage to fall apart. I was just the first one to admit it.

Script #96: Acknowledging One Parent's Emotional Abuse

Yes, it is true that Mom's yelling has something to do with our divorce. But that isn't the only reason. We have both made mistakes that have caused the marriage to be broken. I hope Mom will work on her yelling and will not yell at you, and if you ever feel scared by it, please let me know so I can talk to her. Even when Mom and I make mistakes or lose our tempers, we still love you very much. I promise you that I will do everything I can to make my home for you as calm, safe, and peaceful as possible.

Scripts for Handling an Ex-Abuser Who Continues to Cross Your Boundaries

Even after you have separated or divorced, your former partner may continue pushing the limits, crossing your boundaries, and trying to control you. The anger he or she feels about the break-up may escalate his or her bad behaviors for a time, making things worse before they get better.

A controlling partner may feel completely out-of-control now that you've taken a stand, and he may scramble to reestablish his authority by breaking the newly established house rules or childcare agreements. She may go on a spending spree or attempt to hide money to get back at you. He may say critical things about you to your children, hoping to turn them against you.

It is particularly important during the interim time before a divorce is final or before you or your partner officially split up that you establish firm boundaries and reinforce them every single time they are crossed. This is a time when you may need to implement more serious consequences for

83

his or her behavior, such as creating a legal separation agreement, moving out of the home yourself, blocking phone calls and texts, or changing the locks on the doors.

Even after the divorce, some of these manipulative behaviors may continue, especially if children are involved. Having children together requires that you and your former spouse stay involved in each other's lives, at least until the children are grown.

It's in your best interest to minimize interactions and contact with your former partner, if his or her abusive patterns persist, and to share as little as possible about your new life with him or her. It is even more important that you continue to protect your children from abusive behavior and to provide a safe, peaceful, loving home environment for them to return to if you share custody with your abusive partner.

Script #97: Abuser Disparaging You with Kids

I want you to stop saying ugly things about me to the children. You are putting them in the position of choosing sides, and that is harmful for their emotional well-being. You may think this is my fault, but I am still their mother (or father), and it only hurts them when you disparage me.

Script #98: Abuser Sleeping in Your Bed after Separation

We have agreed to sleep in separate bedrooms while we are separated. I do not want you sleeping with me in this bed. You are breaking our agreement. Do I need to get the court involved in a legal separation agreement?

Script #99: Abuser Taking Money before Divorce

I see you have taken all our money out of our checking account without telling me. By law, half of our assets are mine, so you need to return the money to the account, or I'll have to get the court involved right away. If the money isn't back in the account by 2:00 tomorrow afternoon, I'll ask my attorney to file for an immediate hearing about this issue.

Script #100: Abuser Entering Your Home Uninvited

We are separated, and this is my living space even though we still co-own the house. You cannot just walk in any time you wish. If you want to come over, you need to ask me first and knock on the door before you come in. If you can't do that, I will need to make our separation agreement legal.

Script #101: Abuser Harassing You to Reunite

I want you to stop calling and texting me about getting back together. My decision is final. If you don't stop, I will have to block your calls.

Script #102: Abuser Breaking Childcare Agreement

This is now the fourth time you have asked me to pick up the children on your day to have them.

From now on, you will need to make other arrangements if you can't pick them up, because I have made another firm commitment on that day and time.

Script #103: Abuser Still Trying to Control You

We are divorced. You can no longer push me around or tell me what to do. I make my own decisions, so you need to back off and mind your own business.

Script #104: Abuser Still Demanding

We are no longer married, and I am not on call to help you repair things around the house. You need to hire someone else to do those things for you. Please don't call me about these things any more.

Script #105: Abuser Entering Your Home and Yelling

This is my house, and you may not yell or call me names. Please leave right now. If you don't, I will call the police.

Script #106: Abuser Playing Guilt Card

I am sorry you are unhappy and depressed, but you need to find a counselor or friend to talk to about it and stop calling me. I can no longer be your sounding board. Neither can the children. You are responsible for your own happiness.

Script #107: Final Goodbye to Abuser

I am finally self-confident, happy, and free from your controlling behaviors. I am completely over you. I only wish you happiness, but we are no longer part of each other's lives, and there is no reason for us to continue to communicate. I wish you well. Goodbye.

Barrie Davenport

Conclusion

Learning to speak your mind and stand up for yourself is one of the most valuable skills you will ever learn, and your abusive relationship is certainly the most intense and challenging training laboratory possible for developing these skills. I know you'd prefer to learn them another way, but if there is any gift to be claimed from this heartbreaking relationship dynamic, perhaps this learning opportunity is it.

If you are able to find your voice and build your confidence with an emotionally abusive partner, you'll be empowered for any future situations in life that require inner strength, firm communication, and a lot of emotional discomfort. You will have a PhD in fortitude and courage!

Remember, it is far more important for your own healing and personal growth that you are able to speak up and call your partner out on the abuse than it is for your abuser to react appropriately. You can't force your partner to change. You can only change how you respond to the abuse. By speaking up consistently with mature communication, confidence, and strength, you'll be in a much better frame of mind to make decisions about your relationship and your future.

This strength and confidence doesn't happen overnight. You will falter and slip back into old patterns. Your voice might quiver, you may forget what you want to say, and your abuser may scoff at you or yell over you as you speak. It may feel like you are dying when you demand your rightful place in the relationship. For a period of time, you may need to "act" as you make your statements, communicate your boundaries, and enforce your consequences.

You may need to give the performance of a lifetime, behaving as though you are a confident, secure version of yourself who no longer allows abusive behaviors and words to remain unchecked. Eventually, your true feelings will catch up to your performance. Keep at it, stay committed to calling out the abuse every time it happens, follow through on consequences, and reward positive change with positive comments. Don't expect even a highly motivated abuser to turn things around quickly. It will take a lot of work, patience, and commitment from both of you. Much of this work should be done with a trained and licensed therapist.

It is my sincere hope for you that you see yourself as a person worthy of love, respect, kindness, and intimacy, and that you accept nothing less in your relationship. Even when the consequences of demanding this kind of partnership seem daunting, I hope you recognize that nothing in life is worth sacrificing your mental and emotional health. Not money. Not security. Not your home. Not sex. Not appearances. Not friendships. Not the status quo. Not religious views. Not your reputation. Not even your love for your abuser. You will survive the loss of these things, but you will lose your soul if you sell it to an abusive partner who drains away your self-esteem and identity.

If you need more support and information about emotional abuse and how to deal with it in your intimate relationship, please read my other book on the topic, *Emotional Abuse Breakthrough: How to Speak Up, Set Boundaries, and Break the Cycle of Manipulation and Control with Your Abusive Partner.*

Please visit my site, Live Bold and Bloom.com, for more practical articles and information giving you strategies for living a confident, authentic life. Also, I'd love to hear your feedback on this book and how it's impacted your situation. You can email me at mybloomlife@gmail.com.

Barrie Davenport

Support Resources

Emotional Abuse Breakthrough Course
(http://emotionallyabused.com/)

Find a Therapist
(https://therapists.psychologytoday.com/rms/)

Breakthrough Behavioral, Inc. online therapy
(https://www.breakthrough.com/)

HelpGuide.org, resource for mental, emotional,
and social health
(http://www.helpguide.org/)

WomensHealth.gov
(http://womenshealth.gov/)

Facebook Emotional Abuse Awareness
support group
(https://www.facebook.com/groups/18628385831/?f
ref=ts)

Facebook Emotional Abuse support group
(https://www.facebook.com/groups/2863330782000
34/?fref=ts)

Barrie Davenport

The National Domestic Violence Hotline
1-800-799-SAFE (7233)
1-800-787-3224 (TTY)
(http://www.thehotline.org/)

Childhelp National Child Abuse Hotline
1-800-4-A-CHILD (1-800-442-4453)
(https://www.childhelp.org/hotline/)

Want to Learn More?

If you'd like to learn more about emotional abuse,
healthy relationships, confidence, and self-esteem,
please visit my blog, Live Bold and Bloom.com, and
check out my course, Emotional Abuse
Breakthrough.

Barrie Davenport

Did You Like
Emotional Abuse Breakthrough Scripts?

Thank you so much for purchasing *Emotional Abuse Breakthrough Scripts: 107 Empowering Responses and Boundaries to Use with Your Abuser*. I'm honored by the trust you've placed in me and my work by choosing this book to better understand emotional abuse and try to end it in your relationship. I truly hope you've enjoyed it and found it useful for your life.

I'd like to ask you for a small favor. Would you please take just a minute to leave a review for this book on Amazon? This feedback will help me continue to write the kind of books that will best serve you. If you really loved the book, please let me know!

Barrie Davenport

Other Books You Might Enjoy from Barrie Davenport

Emotional Abuse Breakthrough: How to Speak Up, Set Boundaries, and Break the Cycle of Manipulation and Control with Your Abusive Partner (liveboldandbloom.com/eab-book)

Building Confidence: Get Motivated, Overcome Social Fear, Be Assertive, and Empower Your Life for Success (liveboldandbloom.com/building-confidence)

Peace of Mindfulness: Everyday Rituals to Conquer Anxiety and Claim Unlimited Inner Peace (liveboldandbloom.com/mindfulness-post)

Finely Tuned: How to Thrive as a Highly Sensitive Person or Empath (liveboldandbloom.com/finely-tuned)

201 Relationship Questions: The Couple's Guide to Building Trust and Emotional Intimacy (liveboldandbloom.com/201-questions)

Self-Discovery Questions: 155 Breakthrough Questions to Accelerate Massive Action (liveboldandbloom.com/questions-book)

Confidence Hacks: 99 Small Actions to Massively Boost Your Confidence (liveboldandbloom.com/confidence-hacks)

10-Minute Declutter: The Stress-Free Habit for Simplifying Your Home (liveboldandbloom.com/10-min-declutter)

10-Minute Digital Declutter: The Simple Habit to Eliminate Technology Overload (liveboldandbloom.com/digital-declutter)

Declutter Your Mind: How to Stop Worrying, Relieve Anxiety, and Eliminate Negative Thinking (liveboldandbloom.com/declutter-mind)

Sticky Habits: 6 Simple Steps to Create Good Habits That Stick (liveboldandbloom.com/habitbook)

The 52-Week Life Passion Project: Uncover Your Life Passion (liveboldandbloom.com/life-passion-book)